ACAS code of practice 3

GH00853267

time off
for trade union duties
and activities

First published 1991
Revised 1997

ISBN 0 11 781840 2

This revised Code from pages 6 to 24 revises the *ACAS Code of Practice on Time Off for Trade Union Duties and Activities* which came into effect on 13 May 1991 and was issued under section 6 of the Employment Protection Act 1975 (now section 199 of the Trade Union and Labour Relations (Consolidation) Act 1992 ("the 1992 Act")).

This revised Code is issued under section 201 of the 1992 Act and was laid before both Houses of Parliament on 28 October 1997. The Code comes into effect by order of the Secretary of State on 5 February 1998.

In accordance with section 201, this revised Code makes minor changes only to the earlier Code in order to bring it into conformity with statutory provisions subsequent to that Code.

Contents

Introduction

1. Under section 199 of the Trade Union and Labour Relations (Consolidation) Act 1992 the Advisory, Conciliation and Arbitration Service (ACAS) has a duty to provide practical guidance on the time off to be permitted by an employer:

   (a) to a trade union official in accordance with section 168 of the Trade Union and Labour Relations (Consolidation) Act 1992; and

   (b) to a trade union member in accordance with section 170 of the Trade Union and Labour Relations (Consolidation) Act 1992.

   This Code, which replaces the Code of Practice issued by the Service in 1991, is intended to provide such guidance.

The background

2. The Employment Protection Act 1975 gave trade union officials a statutory right to reasonable paid time off from employment to carry out trade union duties and to undertake trade union training. Union officials and members were also given a statutory right to reasonable unpaid time off when taking part in trade union activities. These rights were subsequently re-enacted as sections 27 and 28 of the Employment Protection (Consolidation) Act 1978 and then as sections 168 - 170 of the Trade Union and Labour Relations (Consolidation) Act 1992.

3. Section 14 of the Employment Act 1989, which came into force on 26th February 1990, and which is now consolidated into

section 168 of the Trade Union and Labour Relations (Consolidation) Act 1992 amended the statutory provisions. In particular, it introduced restrictions on the range of issues for which paid time off for trade union duties can be claimed to those covered by recognition agreements between employers and trade unions. Additionally union duties must relate to the official's own employer and not, for example, to any associated employer.

General purpose of the Code

4. The general purpose of the statutory provisions and this Code of Practice is to aid and improve the effectiveness of relationships between employers and trade unions. Employers and unions have a joint responsibility to ensure that agreed arrangements seek to specify how reasonable time off for union duties and activities and for training can work to their mutual advantage.

Structure of the Code

5. Section 1 of this Code provides guidance on time off for trade union duties. Section 2 deals with time off for training of trade union officials. Section 3 considers time off for trade union activities. In each case the amount and frequency of time off, and the purposes for which and any conditions subject to which time off may be taken, are to be those that are reasonable in all the circumstances. Section 4 describes the responsibilities which employers and trade unions share in considering reasonable time off. Section 5 notes the advantages of reaching formal agreements on time off. Section 6 deals with industrial action and section 7 with methods of appeal.

6. The annex to this Code reproduces the relevant statutory provisions on time off. To help differentiate between these and practical guidance, the summary of statutory provisions relating to time off which appears in the main text of the Code is in **bold type**. Practical guidance is in ordinary type. While every effort has been made to ensure that the summary of the statutory provisions included in this Code is accurate, only the courts can interpret the law authoritatively.

Status of the Code

7. The provisions of this Code are admissible in evidence and may be taken into account in determining any question arising during industrial tribunal proceedings relating to time off for trade union duties and activities. However, failure to observe any provision of the Code does not of itself render a person liable to any proceedings.

Section 1 – TIME OFF FOR TRADE UNION DUTIES

Entitlement

8. Employees who are officials of an independent trade union recognised by their employer are to be permitted reasonable time off during working hours to carry out certain trade union duties.

9. An official is an employee who has been elected or appointed in accordance with the rules of the union to be a representative of all or some of the union's members in the particular company or workplace.

10. Officials are entitled to time off where the duties are concerned with:

    - negotiations with the employer about matters which fall within section 178(2) of the Trade Union and Labour Relations (Consolidation) Act 1992 (TULR(C)A) and for which the union is recognised for the purposes of collective bargaining by the employer; or

    - any other functions on behalf of employees of the employer which are related to matters falling within section 178(2) TULR(C)A and which the employer has agreed the union may perform.

    Matters falling within section 178(2) TULR(C)A are listed in the sub-headings of paragraph 12 below.

11. An independent trade union is recognised by an employer when it is recognised to any extent for the purposes of collective bargaining. Where a trade union is not so recognised by an employer, employees have no statutory right to time off to undertake any duties.

Examples of trade union duties

12. Subject to the recognition or other agreement, trade union officials should be allowed to take reasonable time off for duties concerned with negotiations or, where their employer has agreed, for duties concerned with other functions related to or connected with:

(a) **terms and conditions of employment, or the physical conditions in which workers are required to work.** Examples could include:
    - pay
    - hours of work
    - holidays and holiday pay
    - sick pay arrangements
    - pensions
    - vocational training
    - equal opportunities
    - notice periods
    - the working environment
    - utilisation of machinery and other equipment;

(b) **engagement or non-engagement, or termination or suspension of employment or the duties of employment, of one or more workers.** Examples could include:

- recruitment and selection policies
- human resource planning
- redundancy and dismissal arrangements;

(c) **allocation of work or the duties of employment as between workers or groups of workers.** Examples could include:
- job grading
- job evaluation
- job descriptions
- flexible working practices;

(d) **matters of discipline.** Examples could include:
- disciplinary procedures
- arrangements for representing trade union members at internal interviews
- arrangements for appearing on behalf of trade union members, or as witnesses, before agreed outside appeal bodies or industrial tribunals;

(e) **trade union membership or non-membership.** Examples could include:
- representational arrangements
- any union involvement in the induction of new workers;

(f) **facilities for officials of trade unions.** Examples could include any agreed arrangements for the provision of:
- accommodation
- equipment
- names of new workers to the union;

(g) **machinery for negotiation or consultation and other procedures.** Examples could include arrangements for:
- collective bargaining
- grievance procedures
- joint consultation
- communicating with members
- communicating with other union officials also concerned with collective bargaining with the employer.

13. The duties of an official of a recognised trade union must be connected with or related to negotiations or the performance of functions both in time and subject matter. Reasonable time off may be sought, for example, to:
- prepare for negotiations
- inform members of progress
- explain outcomes to members
- prepare for meetings with the employer about matters for which the trade union has only representational rights.

Payment for time off for trade union duties

14. An employer who permits officials time off for trade union duties must pay them for the time off taken. The employer must pay either the amount that the officials would have earned had they worked during the time off taken or, where earnings vary with the work done, an amount calculated by reference to the average hourly earnings for the work they are employed to do. There is no statutory requirement to pay for time off where the duty is carried out at a time when the official would not otherwise have been at work.

Section 2 – TRAINING OF OFFICIALS IN ASPECTS OF INDUSTRIAL RELATIONS

Entitlement

15. Employees who are officials of an independent trade union recognised by their employer are to be permitted reasonable time off during working hours to undergo training relevant to the carrying out of their trade union duties.[1] These duties must be concerned with:

    - negotiations with the employer about matters which fall within section 178(2) TULR(C)A and for which the union is recognised to any extent for the purposes of collective bargaining by the employer; or

    - any other functions on behalf of employees of the employer which are related to matters falling within section 178(2) TULR(C)A and which the employer has agreed the union may perform.

    Matters falling within section 178(2) TULR(C)A are set out in paragraph 12 above.

What is relevant industrial relations training?

16. **Training should be in aspects of industrial relations relevant to the duties of an official.** There is no one recommended syllabus for training as an official's duties will vary according to:

---

[1]   Section 1 of this Code gives a more complete summary of the statutory entitlement of officials to time off to undertake trade union duties.

- the collective bargaining arrangements at the place of work, particularly the scope of the recognition or other agreement
- the structure of the union
- the role of the official.

17. **The training must also be approved by the Trades Union Congress or by the independent trade union of which the employee is an official.**

18. Trade union officials are more likely to carry out their duties effectively if they possess skills and knowledge relevant to their duties. In particular, employers should be prepared to consider releasing trade union officials for initial training in basic representational skills as soon as possible after their election or appointment, bearing in mind that suitable courses may be infrequent. Reasonable time off could also be considered, for example:

- for further training particularly where the official has special responsibilities
- where there are proposals to change the structure and topics of negotiation about matters for which the union is recognised; or where significant changes in the organisation of work are being contemplated
- where legislative change may affect the conduct of industrial relations at the place of work and may require the reconsideration of existing agreements.

Payment for time off for training

19. An employer who permits time off for officials to attend training relevant to their duties at the workplace must pay them for the time off taken. The employer must pay either the amount that the officials would have earned had they worked during the time off taken or, where earnings vary with the work done, an amount calculated by reference to the average hourly earnings for the work that they are employed to do. There is no statutory requirement to pay for time off where training is undertaken at a time when the official would not otherwise have been at work.

Section 3 – TIME OFF FOR TRADE UNION ACTIVITIES

Entitlement

20. To operate effectively and democratically, trade unions need the active participation of members. It can also be very much in employers' interests that such participation is assured. **An employee who is a member of an independent trade union recognised by the employer in respect of that description of employee is to be permitted reasonable time off during working hours to take part in any trade union activity.**

What are examples of trade union activities?

21. The activities of a trade union member can be, for example:
   - attending workplace meetings to discuss and vote on the outcome of negotiations with the employer
   - meeting full-time officials to discuss issues relevant to the workplace
   - voting in union elections.

22. Where the member is acting as a representative of a recognised union activities can be, for example, taking part in:
   - branch, area or regional meetings of the union where the business of the union is under discussion
   - meetings of official policy making bodies such as the executive committee or annual conference
   - meetings with full-time officials to discuss issues relevant to the workplace.

23. There is no right to time off for trade union activities which themselves consist of industrial action.

Payment for time off for trade union activities

24. There is no requirement that union members or representatives be paid for time off taken on trade union activities. Nevertheless employers may want to consider payment in certain circumstances, for example to ensure that workplace meetings are fully representative.

Section 4 – THE RESPONSIBILITIES OF EMPLOYERS AND TRADE UNIONS

General considerations

25. **The amount and frequency of time off should be reasonable in all the circumstances.** Although the statutory provisions apply to all employers without exception as to size and type of business or service, trade unions should be aware of the wide variety of difficulties and operational requirements to be taken into account when seeking or agreeing arrangements for time off, for example:

    * the size of the organisation and the number of workers
    * the production process
    * the need to maintain a service to the public
    * the need for safety and security at all times.

26. Employers in turn should have in mind the difficulties for trade union officials and members in ensuring effective representation and communications with, for example:
    * shift workers
    * part-time workers
    * those employed at dispersed locations
    * workers with particular domestic commitments.

27. For time off arrangements to work satisfactorily trade unions should:

    * ensure that officials are aware of their role, responsibilities and functions

- inform management, in writing, as soon as possible of appointments or resignations of officials
- ensure that officials receive any appropriate written credentials promptly.

28. Employers should consider making available to officials the facilities necessary for them to perform their duties efficiently and communicate effectively with their members, fellow lay officials and full-time officers. Where resources permit the facilities could include:
    - accommodation for meetings
    - access to a telephone and other office equipment
    - the use of notice boards
    - where the volume of the official's work justifies it, the use of dedicated office space.

Requesting time off

29. Trade union officials and members requesting time off to pursue their industrial relations duties or activities should provide management with as much notice as possible and give details of:
    - the purpose of such time off
    - the intended location
    - the timing and duration of time off required.

30. In addition, officials who request paid time off to undergo relevant training should:
    - give at least a few weeks' notice to management of nominations for training courses
    - if asked to do so, provide a copy of the syllabus or prospectus indicating the contents of the training course.

31. When deciding whether requests for paid time off should be granted, consideration would need to be given as to their reasonableness, for example to ensure adequate cover for safety or to safeguard the production process or the provision of service. Similarly managers and unions should seek to agree a mutually convenient time which minimises the effect on production or services. Where workplace meetings are requested consideration should be given to holding them, for example:

    - towards the end of a shift or the working week
    - before or after a meal break.

32. Employers need to consider each application for time off on its merits; they might also need to consider the reasonableness of the request in relation to agreed time off already taken or in prospect.

Section 5 – AGREEMENTS ON TIME OFF

33. To take account of the wide variety of circumstances and problems which can arise, there can be positive advantages for employers and trade unions in establishing agreements on time off in ways which reflect their own situations. A formal agreement can help to:

    - provide clear guidelines against which applications for time off can be determined
    - avoid misunderstanding
    - facilitate better planning
    - ensure fair and reasonable treatment.

34. Agreements could specify:

    - the amount of time off permitted
    - the occasions on which time off can be taken
    - in what circumstances time off will be paid
    - to whom time off will be paid
    - the procedure for requesting time off.

35. In addition, it would be sensible for agreements to make clear:

    - arrangements for the appropriate payment to be made when time off relates in part to union duties and in part to union activities
    - whether payment (to which there would be no statutory entitlement) might be made to shift and part-time employees undertaking trade union duties outside their normal working hours.

36. Agreements for time off and other facilities for union representation should be consistent with wider agreements which deal with such matters as constituencies, number of representatives and the election of officials.

37. In smaller organisations, it might be thought more appropriate for employers and unions to reach understandings about how requests for time off are to be made; and more broadly to agree flexible arrangements which can accommodate their particular circumstances.

38. The absence of a formal agreement on time off, however, does not in itself deny an individual any statutory entitlement. Nor does any agreement supersede statutory entitlement to time off.

Section 6 – INDUSTRIAL ACTION

39. Employers and unions have a responsibility to use agreed procedures to settle problems and avoid industrial action. Time off may therefore be permitted for this purpose particularly where there is a dispute. **There is no right to time off for trade union activities which themselves consist of industrial action.** However, where an official is not taking part in industrial action but represents members involved, normal arrangements for time off with pay for the official should apply.

Section 7 - MAKING A COMPLAINT

40. Every effort should be made to resolve any dispute or grievance in relation to time off work for union duties or activities. There is advantage in agreeing ways in which such disputes can be settled and any appropriate procedures to resolve disputes should be followed. **Where the grievance remains unresolved, trade union officials or members have a right to complain to an industrial tribunal that their employer has failed to allow reasonable time off or, in the case of an official, has failed to pay for all or part of the time off taken. Such complaints may be resolved by conciliation by ACAS and, if this is successful, no tribunal hearing will be necessary.** ACAS assistance may also be sought without the need for a formal complaint to a tribunal.

Annex – THE LAW ON TIME OFF FOR TRADE UNION DUTIES AND ACTIVITIES

Section 168 of the Trade Union and Labour Relations (Consolidation) Act 1992 states:

(1) An employer shall permit an employee of his who is an official of an independent trade union recognised by the employer to take time off during his working hours for the purpose of carrying out any duties of his, as such an official, concerned with -

(a) negotiations with the employer related to or connected with matters falling within section 178(2) (collective bargaining) in relation to which the trade union is recognised by the employer, or

(b) the performance on behalf of employees of the employer of functions related to or connected with matters falling within that provision which the employer has agreed may be so performed by the trade union.

(2) He shall also permit such an employee to take time off during his working hours for the purpose of undergoing training in aspects of industrial relations -

(a) relevant to the carrying out of such duties as are mentioned in subsection (1), and

(b) approved by the Trades Union Congress or by the independent trade union of which he is an official.

(3) The amount of time off which an employee is to be permitted to take under this section and the purposes for which, the occasions on which and any conditions subject to which time off may be so taken are those that are reasonable in all the circumstances having regard to any relevant provisions of a Code of Practice issued by ACAS.

(4) An employee may present a complaint to an industrial tribunal that his employer has failed to permit him to take time off as required by this section.

Section 169 of the Trade Union and Labour Relations (Consolidation) Act 1992 states:

(1) An employer who permits an employee to take time off under section 168 shall pay him for the time taken off pursuant to the permission.

(2) Where the employee's remuneration for the work he would ordinarily have been doing during that time does not vary with the amount of work done, he shall be paid as if he had worked at that work for the whole of that time.

(3) Where the employee's remuneration for the work he would ordinarily have been doing during that time varies with the amount of work done, he shall be paid an amount calculated by reference to the average hourly earnings for that work.

The average hourly earnings shall be those of the employee concerned or, if no fair estimate can be made of those earnings, the average hourly earnings for work of that description of persons in comparable employment with the same employer or, if there are no such persons, a figure of average hourly earnings which is reasonable in the circumstances.

(4) A right to be paid an amount under this section does not affect any right of an employee in relation to remuneration under his contract of employment, but -

   (a) any contractual remuneration paid to an employee in respect of a period of time off to which this section applies shall go towards discharging any liability of the employer under this section in respect of that period, and

   (b) any payment under this section in respect of a period shall go towards discharging any liability of the employer to pay contractual remuneration in respect of that period.

(5) An employee may present a complaint to an industrial tribunal that his employer has failed to pay him in accordance with this section.

Section 170 of the Trade Union and Labour Relations (Consolidation) Act 1992 states:

(1) An employer shall permit an employee of his who is a member of an independent trade union recognised by the employer in respect of that description of employee to take time off during his working hours for the purpose of taking part in -

   (a) any activities of the union, and

   (b) any activities, in relation to which the employee is acting as a representative of the union.

(2) The right conferred by subsection (1) does not extend to
activities which themselves consist of industrial action, whether
or not in contemplation or furtherance of a trade dispute.

(3) The amount of time off which an employee is to be permitted to
take under this section and the purposes for which, the occasions
on which and any conditions subject to which time off may be so
taken are those that are reasonable in all the circumstances
having regard to any relevant provisions of a Code of Practice
issued by ACAS.

(4) An employee may present a complaint to an industrial tribunal
that his employer has failed to permit him to take time off as
required by this section.

Section 178(1) - (3) of the Trade Union and Labour Relations (Consolidation) Act 1992 states:

(1) In this Act "collective agreement" means any agreement or
arrangement made by or on behalf of one or more trade unions
and one or more employers or employers' associations and
relating to one or more of the matters specified below; and
"collective bargaining" means negotiations relating to or
connected with one or more of those matters.

(2) The matters referred to above are -

(a) terms and conditions of employment, or the physical
conditions in which any workers are required to work;

(b) engagement or non-engagement, or termination or
    suspension of employment or the duties of employment, of
    one or more workers;

(c) allocation of work or the duties of employment as between
    workers or groups of workers;

(d) matters of discipline;

(e) a worker's membership or non-membership of a trade union;

(f) facilities for officials of trade unions; and

(g) machinery for negotiation or consultation, and other
    procedures, relating to any of the above matters, including
    the recognition by employers or employers' associations of
    the right of a trade union to represent workers in such
    negotiation or consultation or in the carrying out of such
    procedures.

(3) In this Act "recognition", in relation to a trade union, means the
    recognition of the union by an employer, or two or more
    associated employers, to any extent, for the purpose of collective
    bargaining; and "recognised" and other related expressions shall
    be construed accordingly.

Section 173(1) of the Trade Union and Labour Relations (Consolidation) Act 1992 states:

For the purposes of sections 168 and 170 the working hours of an
employee shall be taken to be any time when in accordance with his
contract of employment he is required to be at work.

Section 119 of the Trade Union and Labour Relations (Consolidation) Act 1992 states:
"Official" means -

(a) an officer of the union or of a branch or section of the union, or

(b) a person elected or appointed in accordance with the rules of the union to be a representative of its members or of some of them,

and includes a person so elected or appointed who is an employee of the same employer as the members or one or more of the members whom he is to represent.

Useful information

The right to paid time off for employees who seek election as, or who carry out the functions of, employee representatives for the purposes of consultation on collective redundancies and on business transfers (found in section 61 of the Employment Rights Act 1996) falls outside the scope of the Code of Practice on Time Off for Trade Union Duties and Activities. More information about these rights can be found in the following Department of Trade and Industry publications:

Redundancy consultation and notification PL833 Rev 4 (collective redundancies)
Employment rights on transfer of an undertaking PL699 Rev 3 (business transfers)

Published by the Stationery Office and available from:

The Publications Centre
(mail, telephone and fax orders only)
PO Box 276, London SW8 5DT
General enquiries 0171 873 0011
Telephone orders 0171 873 9090
Fax orders 0171 873 8200

The Stationery Office Bookshops
59-60 Holborn Viaduct, London EC1A 2FD
temporary until mid 1998
(counter service and fax orders only)
Fax 0171 831 1326
68-69 Bull Street, Birmingham B4 6AD
0121 236 9696 Fax 0121 236 9699
33 Wine Street, Bristol BS1 2BQ
0117 926 4306 Fax 0117 929 4515
9-21 Princess Street, Manchester M60 8AS
0161 834 7201 Fax 0161 833 0634

16 Arthur Street, Belfast BT1 4GD
01232 238451 Fax 01232 235401
The Stationery Office Oriel Bookshop
The Friary, Cardiff CF1 4AA
01222 395548 Fax 01222 384347
71 Lothian Road, Edinburgh EH3 9AZ
(counter service only)

Customers in Scotland may
mail, telephone or fax their orders to:
Scottish Publications Sales
South Gyle Crescent, Edinburgh EH12 9EB
0131 622 7050 Fax 0131 622 7017

The Stationery Office's Accredited Agents
(see Yellow Pages)

ACAS Reader Ltd
PO Box 16, Earl Shilton, Leicester LE9 8ZZ
01455 8252225

and through good booksellers

ACAS Public Enquiry Points

Birmingham	Tel: (0121) 622 5050
Bristol	Tel: (0117) 974 4066
Cardiff	Tel: (01222) 761126
Fleet	Tel: (01252) 811868
Glasgow	Tel: (0141) 204 2677
Leeds	Tel: (0113) 243 1371
Liverpool	Tel: (0151) 427 8881
London	Tel: (0171) 396 5100
Manchester	Tel: (0161) 228 3222
Newcastle upon Tyne	Tel: (0191) 261 2191
Nottingham	Tel: (0115) 969 3355

ACAS main offices

Midlands Region
Leonard House, 319/323 Bradford Street, Birmingham B5 6ET

Anderson House, Clinton Avenue, Nottingham NG5 1AW

Northern Region
Commerce House, St Alban's Place, Leeds LS2 8HH

Westgate House, Westgate Road, Newcastle upon Tyne NE1 1TJ

North West Region
Boulton House, 17-21 Chorlton Street, Manchester M1 3HY

Cressington House, 249 St Mary's Road, Garston, Liverpool L19 0NF

South and West Region
Regent House, 27a Regent Street, Clifton, Bristol BS8 4HR

Westminster House, Fleet Road, Fleet, Hants GU13 8PD

London, Eastern and Southern Area
Clifton House, 83-117 Euston Road, London NW1 2RB

39 King Street, Thetford, Norfolk IP24 2AU

Suites 3-5, Business Centre, 1-7 Commercial Road, Paddock Wood, Kent TN12 6EN

Scotland
Franborough House, 123-157 Bothwell Street, Glasgow G2 7JR

Wales
3 Purbeck House, Lambourne Crescent, Llanishen, Cardiff CF4 5GJ

Head Office
Brandon House, 180 Borough High Street, London SE1 1LW

INVESTORS IN PEOPLE

ISBN 0-11-781840-2

9 780117 818408